Life Cycle of a

Dog

Angela Royston

Heinemann Library
Chicago, Illinois

Designed by Celia Floyd
Illustrated by Alan Fraser
Printed in China by South China Printing Co. Ltd.

04 03 02 01
10 9 8 7 6 5 4 3 2

Library of Congress Cataloging-in-Publication Data
Royston, Angela.
    Life cycle of a dog / Angela Royston.
        p. cm.
    Includes bibliographical references (p.) and index.
    Summary: Introduces the life cycle of a dog, using a golden retriever as an example and describing various stages of her life, from newborn puppy to adult dog having puppies of her own.
    ISBN 1-57572-209-7 (lib. bdg.)
    1. Dogs—Life cycles—Juvenile literature. [1. Dogs.] I. Title.

SF426.5.R69 2000
636.752'7—dc21   99-046854

Acknowledgments
The Publisher would like to thank the following for permission to reproduce photographs:

Ardea London/John Daniels, pp. 7, 8, 9, 10, 20, 21, 22, 24, 26; FLPA/B. S. Turner, p. 17; FLPA/David Hosking, pp. 18, 19; FLPA/Foto Natura, p. 25; FLPA/Gerard Lacz, p. 23, FLPA/H. D. Brandl, p. 16; FLPA/J. & P. Wegner, p. 5; FLPA/Roger Wilmshurst, p. 27; John Daniels, pp. 11, 15; Marc Henrie Assoc., London, pp. 6, 12, 13, 14; Tony Stone/Tim Davis, p. 4.

Cover photograph: Bruce Coleman

Every effort has been made to contact copyright holders of any material reproduced in this book. Any omissions will be rectified in subsequent printings if notice is given to the Publisher.

Some words are shown in bold, **like this.** You can find out what they mean by looking in the glossary.

Contents

Meet the Dogs

There are hundreds of different kinds of dogs. This picture shows a basset hound, a golden retriever, and a tiny chihuahua.

Newborn

Six weeks

Eight weeks

This book tells you about the life of
a female golden retriever. She has
floppy ears and a long tail. She
began life as a tiny puppy.

One year

Three years

Old age

Newborn

The mother dog has given birth to a **litter** of puppies. The little female puppy is the last to be born. She has lots of brothers and sisters.

Newborn

Six weeks

Eight weeks

The **newborn** puppy cannot see
or hear, but she can feel and smell.
She smells her mother and the
other puppies in the litter.

One year

Three years

Old age

Feeding

The puppy is one week old. She feeds on her mother's milk. She has to push between her brothers and sisters to find room to drink.

Newborn

Six weeks

Eight weeks

The puppies feed and grow bigger.
They still cannot stand. They
snuggle up together and sleep.

One year   Three years   Old age

Walking and Playing

Now the puppy is six weeks old.
Her eyes have opened. She can see
and hear. Her legs are strong now,
so she can run and play.

Newborn   Six weeks   Eight weeks

She plays with her brothers and sisters. Sometimes she pretends to fight with one of them. In this way, the puppies learn who is stronger.

One year

Three years

Old age

Exploring

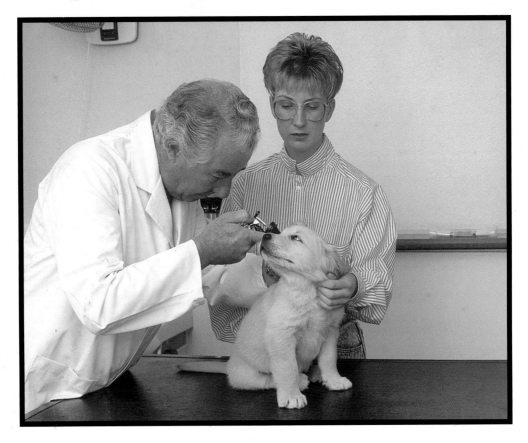

The **vet** gives the puppy a checkup.
He gives her a special **injection**.
The **vaccines** will keep her from
catching dangerous **diseases.**

Newborn

Six weeks

Eight weeks

The puppy can now go outside for the first time. Everything is strange. She has a good sense of smell and uses it to explore.

One year

Three years

Old age

Growing Up

At eight weeks, the dog leaves her mother and goes to a new owner. She can eat puppy food now instead of milk.

Newborn

Six weeks

Eight weeks

The food gives her **energy** and keeps her healthy. Exercise makes her muscles stronger. She plays with other dogs she meets outside.

One year   Three years   Old age

Fully Grown

The dog is now one year old. She is fully grown and has lots of **energy**. When her owner throws a stick, she runs and brings it back.

Newborn

Six weeks

Eight weeks

To retrieve means to bring back.
Retrievers can be **trained** to do
work and help people. Some are
specially trained to be **guide dogs**.

One year Three years Old age

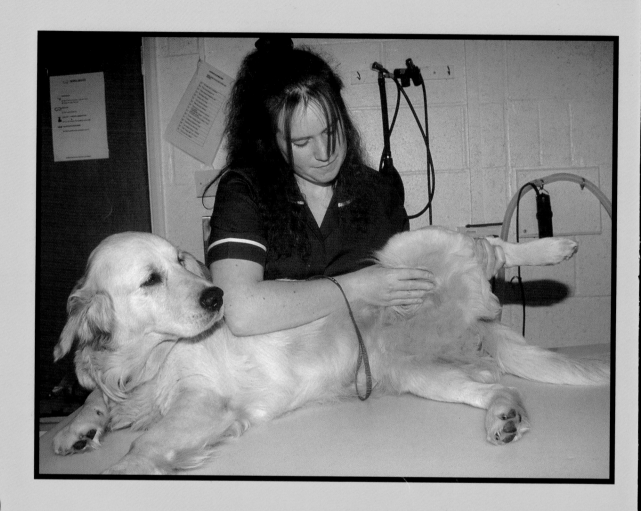

The dog goes to the **vet** every year. The vet takes her pulse and makes sure that she is healthy.

Newborn

Six weeks

Eight weeks

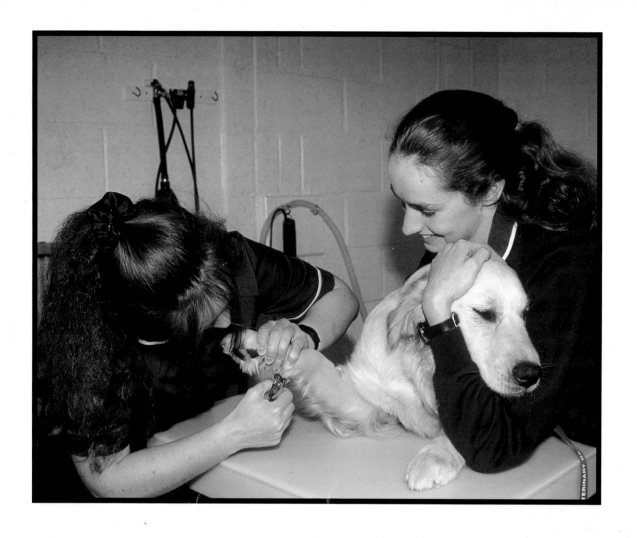

Then she gives the dog a **booster injection** to keep her from getting **diseases.** The vet also clips her nails so they do not get too long.

One year Three years Old age

New Puppies

Now the dog is three years old. Her owner wants her to have puppies of her own. Her owner takes her to **mate** with a male dog.

Newborn Six weeks Eight weeks

Now some puppies are growing
inside her. They stay inside for nine
weeks. Look how big her stomach is!
She is almost ready to **give birth.**

One year   Three years   Old age

The dog **gives birth** to her **litter** of puppies one by one. The puppies are very small. They feed on their mother's milk and grow quickly.

Newborn

Six weeks

Eight weeks

By the time they are three weeks old, they can bark and wag their tails. When they are eight weeks old, the puppies go to new owners.

One year

Three years

Old age

Growing Older

The dog still has lots of **energy,**
but she is calm and well-behaved.
She likes to be with her owners.

Newborn

Six weeks

Eight weeks

They take her for long walks.
When they throw a stick, she runs
after it. She swims through the
water to fetch the stick.

One year

Three years

Old age

Old Age

The dog is eight years old now. She still needs exercise every day, but she walks more slowly now. She does not run around as much.

Newborn

Six weeks

Eight weeks

Most dogs live until they are ten to fifteen years old. Small dogs often live longer than bigger dogs.

One year

Three years

Old age

Life Cycle

Newborn

1

Six weeks

2

Eight weeks

3

One year

4

Three years

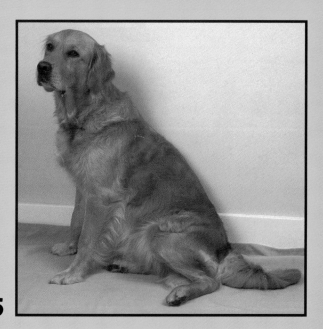

5

Old age

6

Fact File

Dogs are popular pets. There are about 50 million dogs in the United States.

Many retrievers like being in water because their hairy coats are **waterproof**.

Dogs are usually **color-blind**. Most colors look alike to them. But a dog can smell well enough to follow the tracks left by a person's shoes!

Retrievers can have several **litters**. In each litter, they usually have seven to nine puppies.

Glossary

booster   second shot that makes the first shot work better

color-blind not able to see different colors clearly

disease sickness

energy   ability to run around and do things

give birth to have babies

guide dog dog that is specially trained to help people who cannot see or hear well

injection   when medicine is pushed into the body with a special needle—also called a shot

litter   several baby animals born together

newborn just born

trained   taught

vaccine shot of a weak illness used to help your body learn to protect itself (You say vak-SEEN.)

vet   animal doctor, short for veterinarian

waterproof   able to keep out water

More Books to Read

Feldman, Heather H. *The Story of the Golden Retriever.* New York: Rosen Publishing Group, 1999.

Kallen, Stuart A. *Golden Retrievers.* Minneapolis: ABDO Publishing, 1998.

Patten, John M., Jr. *Sporting Dogs.* Vero Beach, Fla.: Rourke Corporation, 1996.

Wilcox, Charlotte. *The Golden Retriever.* Mankato, Minn.: Capstone Press, 1996.
An older reader can help you with this book.

Index